D1097904

First Loves

Life Stories of Victorian Dolls

by Lilian McCrea

INTRODUCTION

The object of this book is not to add to the vast amount of information already available on Victorian dolls as valuable antiques, works of art and wise investments, but rather to present dolls in their proper setting, as the playthings of children.

It is as playthings that dolls figure in the following stories and anecdotes which I collected over a number of years as important to my collection of Victorian dolls. Some concern dolls in my keeping and were recounted to me by those who had cherished them all their lives; others are the reminiscences of friends whose memories were stirred by the sight of dolls so like the ones with which they themselves once played.

Whether sad or amusing, the stories reflect life as children, both rich and poor, knew it nearly a hundred years ago, revealing their problems, joys and sorrows, fears and doubts.

A wide variety of dolls are involved in the stories, from the poor child's rag baby to the rich child's French beauty, but ugly or beautiful, all were loved. To a child, a doll is real whatever it may look like. Its comfortable presence is all that matters.

Published by Scarthin Books, Cromford, Derbyshire

Phototypesetting, printing by Higham Press Ltd., Shirland, Derbyshire

ISBN 0 907758 12 6

CONTENTS

Belinda with the tell-tale Cheeks
Consumption

A DOLL FOR MY POCKET

In a faded cardboard box, wrapped up in yellowing tissue paper, is a small and beautiful china doll. On the lid, in childish writing, is one word - 'PRIVATE' and accompanying the doll, inside the box, is a note which reads—

My dear Niece,
      I am sending you a small doll
as a present for your birthday.
      I hope you will live to have
very many happy ones, each one to be brighter
than the last.
      I trust I shall be able to
see you all soon.
      With love to all,
        I am
      Your affectionate Uncle
      James Barker.

The 'dear Niece' is now a very old lady, but not too old to remember the story of the little china doll. Here it is as she told it to me.

"I was an only child and very delicate. In spite of my poor health, however, my parents were very strict with me but I had a batchelor uncle who spoiled me. Every time he visited us, and on my birthday and at Christmas, he gave me a present. As this was usually a doll, you may imagine

5

I had a very large family indeed. My dolls sat side by side on a shelf in my nursery and they made a pretty sight, except that some of them had very little hair for I was fond of cutting it off in the interest of their health. You see, in those days, it was commonly believed that if a child's hair was very luxuriant, it must be sapping her strength and it was only wise to cut it off.

I remember all my dolls, but three are outstanding in my memory. One was Victoria, a beautiful wax doll with flaxen curls whom I put to sleep in my doll's cradle. One day, a little puppy we were minding for a friend curled up on top of her with the most dire results. The wax melted and poor Victoria's beauty was gone for ever. She had to be discarded and I was greatly distressed. Another was a baby doll called George which my mother had dressed in a set of clothes which, she said, was an exact replica of one worn by my brother who had died in infancy. I never cared for George because, in my mind he was associated with death and I lived in constant fear of dying myself as I was so often ill. The other doll was Lavinia, the little doll in the box. She arrived on my sixth birthday and I loved her on sight on account of her smallness and the tiny knitted dress she wore. I called her 'Lavinia' because that name came straight into my head as I looked at her. I turned her over in my hands and then, joy of joys, I found she exactly fitted into my pocket. You must know that when I was a child all our frocks had capacious pockets entered through a slit in the skirt. After that, Lavinia lived in my pocket except at night when she slept under my pillow. She shared my whole life, We played together, felt ill together, recovered together; we discussed the possibility of our early demise and had the cosiest conversations about all the dead-and-gone people we would meet again in Heaven. Best of all, Lavinia loved listening to my stories which were not the orthodox ones about Kings and Princes but truly horrible ones about operations, burglars and child snatchers. I still played with my other dolls and enjoyed cutting their hair, but Lavinia was not like them, she was a doll apart.

A Doll For My Pocket

When I was eight, the Doctor decided I was strong enough to go to school. I was very excited about this especially as I was to wear a school uniform. When the great day arrived, my problem was what to do with Lavinia. I could not bear to put her in the nursery with my other dolls when she was not one of them, and I could not put her in my pocket for my uniform had only a flat 'patch' pocket quite unsuitable for holding a doll. I decided I would put her back in her own box which, naturally, I had kept, as we kept everything in those days. So I laid her in the tissue paper and put the box in my handkerchief drawer.

I enjoyed my first day at school. We had a Nature lesson and I was able to point out to the governess that she had misnamed a tree. I promised to take her a book on the subject the next day to prove my point!

When I got home I was told to go upstairs and change my uniform as it was not for playing in. This accomplished, I went into the nursery to play and there a shock awaited me. My dolls had vanished! The shelf was empty! I flew downstairs crying, "Mamma! Mamma! Someone has taken my dolls!"

My mother came into the hall and said in her usual matter-of-fact tones, "It was I. You are too big to play with dolls now, you are a school girl. I have sent them to the Children's Home."

I was nonplussed. I could not speak. I could not cry. My mother showed me no sympathy, that was the way long ago. Things were done for your own good and you were expected to accept them without question.

But I still had Lavinia, and that evening, I took the precaution of writing 'PRIVATE' on the lid of her box. No-one, not even my mother, I thought, would interfere with anything marked 'Private'. And no-one ever did. Lavinia remained safe in her box for evermore. I sought her comfort less and less as the years went by until, at last, like the Princess in the story, she fell asleep for a hundred years — or nearly a hundred years. And now, here she is today, as young and beautiful as ever".

'DUTCH' DOLLS

Small ones cost a penny, large ones a shilling

CONSUMPTION

Ashort distance from where we lived as children was an old house set in a beautiful garden. One memorable day, I think I would have been about seven years old at the time, I was strolling past this house with Mother when she suddenly stopped and peeped over the wall. Then, without a word she lifted me up that I might peep too, and the sight that I saw will live in my memory for ever. The great lawn before the house was an unbroken carpet of crocuses, their mingling colours brilliant in the sunlight. I gazed at the scene enraptured, more moved I am sure, than ever Wordsworth was by his daffodils.

As we resumed our walk, I asked Mother who lived in that magical place. "The Barbers," she replied, adding sadly, "The daughter has consumption."

"How do you know?" I questioned.

"You have only to look at her to know," said Mamma. "She has the tell-tale red cheeks. Extra bright cheeks are a sure sign of consumption." "Will she die?" I asked, pursuing the subject with morbid interest, "Yes," said Mamma, with finality. "There is no cure for consumption."

When we got home, I went into the play-room to play with my dolls. Suddenly I was struck by the fiery redness of Belinda's cheeks. Belinda was my Dutch doll and, as you know, the cheeks of Dutch dolls are just blobs of red paint. With Mamma's words still ringing in my ears, I decided she had consumption.

The next day when I went next-door to play with my friend Joy, I pushed Belinda along in her pram. "How is Belinda today?" asked Joy chattily.

"She's very poorly," I replied. "She has consumption."

"Is that what the Doctor says?" enquired Joy.

I explained that it had not been necessary to have the Doctor to diagnose her condition as her bright red cheeks were indication enough. "She'll die," I finished. "People with consumption always die. There is no cure for it."

Joy looked from Belinda to me and then remarked, "You've got red cheeks. Are you going to die?".

This observation made in all innocence, struck a chill to my heart, and was to haunt me for a long day to come. I knew my cheeks were red because people used to say, "Isn't she bonny!" and this, Mamma had explained was a way of saying I had rosy cheeks. I had never liked my rosy cheeks, because I hated people saying this, but now, I was positively frightened of them. Did they mean I had consumption? Was I really going to die? The thought terrified me.

That night I said to my elder sister Jenny, "Do you know when you're going to die?"

"No," she replied. Then, realising I was expecting more, added, "God decides, and when he has decided He sends an angel down to carry your soul up to Heaven."

Her explanation made me feel worse than ever. I knew about the soul because once, when we were walking through the graveyard, I had asked Mamma how it was that dead people could be buried in the ground and yet be with God in Heaven. She had told me it was their souls that were in Heaven and that only their empty bodies were buried in the ground. From this, I deduced that the soul was a person's inside and that at the appointed time an angel descended to draw it out, leaving the body empty and dead. I wasn't going to let this frightful thing happen to me!

I assumed that angels were only sent about their business in the dark, so that night, and for many nights to follow, I hid from them under the bedclothes with "Evie" my baby doll, held tightly in my arms for comfort. Only when I heard the others coming up to bed, imagining there to be safety in numbers, would I emerge with exquisite relief to breathe the cool, fresh air.

But suddenly, and in a most unexpected way, my fears were vanquished. One night as I lay smothering under the bedclothes with Evie in my arms, I heard Mother and Father coming upstairs, talking as they came. I seized the opportunity to get a breath of air and when I heard them coming

10

into my room, I pretended to be asleep with Evie beside me. They stood by my bed and, I suppose, looked down at the two of us. "I wonder what she'll say when the real baby arrives!" said my father.

"I wonder," said my mother. "She has been the baby for so long."

They went away then and I turned my thoughts to what they had said. Parcels arrived. Letters arrived. Did babies arrive too? "Mamma," I asked next day, "How do you get a baby?",

I expected her to say, "The postman brings it," but instead she said, "God sends it."

"When?" I asked.

"When it's ready," she replied.

"Are we going to get a baby, Mamma?" I persisted.

If she was suspicious that I had overheard the conversation of the night before, she did not show it. All she said was, "I hope so."

I was greatly excited. "When, Mamma?" I asked. "When will it be ready? When will God sent it?"

"Very soon, I hope," she said.

And very soon, a real baby did arrive. It was a little boy, and in my joy in the days that followed, my rosy cheeks, consumption and death were all forgotten.

A LIFE-SIZED RAG BABY

We were a large family and lived in a very pretty cottage in the country which we rented for about half-a-crown a week. We were poor but we were never hungry or cold, and we were always nicely dressed for Mother was an excellent dress-maker and could make even the 'sensible' material which Father always insisted on buying himself, into attractive suits and dresses. However, there was very little money to spare. An annual sixpence when The Fair came to our village for one day in August was all we children ever had to spend. We looked forward to The Fair all the year round and as soon as it was over, we started looking forward to the next.

We had numerous jobs to do such as collecting kindling for the fire, going to the village tap for water and down to the river for it on wash-day, feeding the chickens and collecting the eggs, and picking vegetables and fruit in their season. In addition to all these, my sister and I had an extra job.

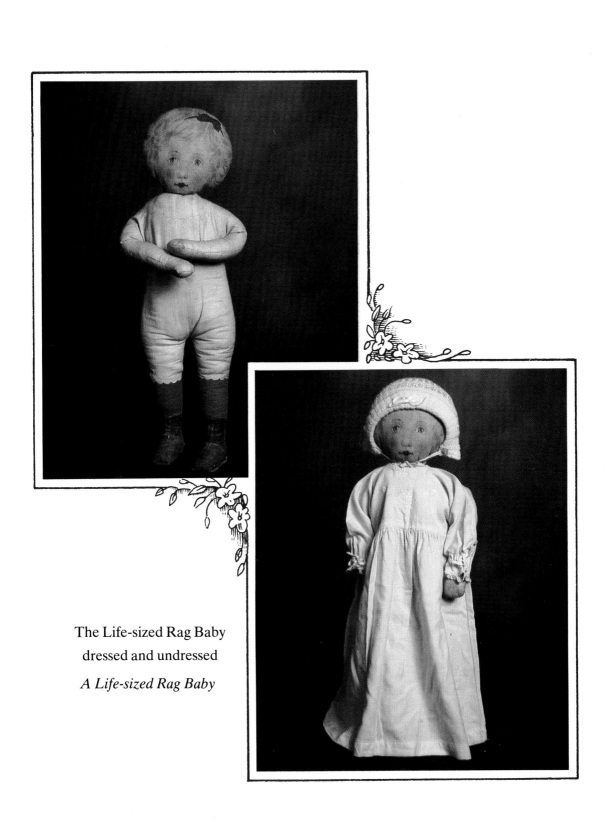

The Life-sized Rag Baby
dressed and undressed

A Life-sized Rag Baby

Every week, one of us had to go to help our Grandmother. This, we detested because Grandma was a cantankerous old woman and nothing we ever did suited her.

With so much work and school as well, you may imagine we had little time to play. But we didn't mind. We played games of magic as we went about our work, jumping over certain stones, running three times round certain rocks and scampering past the 'One - Armed -Woman's' cave before she had a chance to grab us with her one arm! I don't remember playing with toys and I never thought about dolls until we saw the advertisement for the 'Life-Sized Rag Baby' in the paper. I would have been about eight then.

All you had to do to acquire this wonderful baby was to send a postal order for the pattern. It was the words 'life-sized' that attracted me. I may not have wanted a doll before but I had always wanted a baby. I had asked Mother many times why we couldn't have one like other children we knew but the only reply I ever got was, "You are the baby in this House." This seemed an odd answer to me because I was a big girl and babies wore long clothes and were carried about. However, a life-sized baby doll I thought, would surely be almost as good as a real baby. I begged Mother to send for the pattern and, strangely enough, she agreed.

In due course, the pattern arrived and to our astonishment, it depicted, not a new-born baby but a sturdy little girl. She wore red socks and black boots, her under-clothes were sketched in, and her serious little face framed by a quantity of yellow hair. She may not have been what we expected but nevertheless, we all thought her beautiful. Mother cut the pattern out and machined it round, then we all helped to stuff the doll. This was no mean task, and well do I remember the huge blisters which rose on our fingers as, in our excitement, we chopped frantically at the coarse 'bits' Mother considered good enough for that purpose. When it was finished, my brothers observed rudely that it looked like a scarecrow and I must confess I secretly agreed. Also, as we hadn't stuffed the neck very firmly, its over-large head kept flopping about in a most alarming fashion. But when it was dressed in baby clothes, it was transformed. It looked and felt exactly like a real baby. I can't describe the feelings that welled up in me when I took the 'baby' in my arms, feelings of love, pride, motherhood all mixed up together.

That week it was my turn to visit Grandma and I took Baby with me. When my Grandmother opened the door to me, her face at once crumpled into disapproval. "What is the meaning of this?" she snapped. "Bringing a baby with you, what next! Does your mother know? Whose baby is it?".

Obviously, Grandma thought I had a real baby in my arms but I was too frightened to tell her it was only a doll. I was too frightened to speak. Losing patience, she ordered me to put the baby down and get on with my work. As I lowered the doll into a chair, its head flopped forward with such suddenness Grandma's attention was arrested. She peered at the 'baby' and realized it was only a doll. She had been made a fool of! That was too much. She grabbed me by the shoulders and SHOOK me.

I began to cry of course and I cried all the rest of the time I was there. But when I got outside with Baby in my arms, my spirits rose. What did I care about my cross old Grandma, I had a baby, a beautiful baby, a baby all my own. What more could I wish for!

My happiness was complete.

A French Doll from Paris dressed as Millie's Doll
"Molly" and the French Doll

'MOLLY' AND THE FRENCH DOLL

When I was a little girl, I had a doll called Molly and a friend called Millie. The two are coupled in my memory on account of the incident of the French doll.

I loved Molly with all my heart. My Grandmother had given her to me on my birthday when I was two and so we has grown up together. She was a large doll, or so she seemed to me. Her body was agreeably soft and her head and arms and legs were made of some kind of unbreakable material which my mother often remarked was a charity, as she had so many bumps and tumbles.

I do not know if Molly was pretty or not, I paid no heed to her features until the incident of the French doll. This occurred when I was about six. Millie was the same age. We were great friends which was very nice as neither of us had any brothers or sisters. Our mothers were great friends too which was also very nice, because when we were all together they were so engrossed in one another's company, they left us to play unobserved.

One day when I went to play with Millie, accompanied of course by Molly whom I never on any account left behind, I found her in a state of considerable excitement. "You don't know what I'm going to have," she said, "a French doll from Paris! Uncle George is bringing her when he comes to stay".

I had no idea what a 'French doll from Paris' signified but I gathered from Millie's manner it was something special. And so it was. "She has a china face, and can say 'Ma-Ma'," said Millie, "and ringlets of real hair that you can comb. She has a silk frock with a hat to match, leather shoes, silk stockings and GLOVES!"

Obviously, it was the gloves that had touched Millie's fancy for she fairly shouted the word. But it was the ringlets of real hair that touched mine. Imagine a doll with hair that you could comb! For the first time I regarded Mollie with a critical eye. Her hair was only painted on and most of that was worn away. I pictured her with ringlets hanging to her waist and I gently combing them out. I could wash them I thought, and trim them, and tie them up with ribbons. When I returned home I told Mother about the French doll, omitting the details of raiment and dwelling only on the ringlets. Mamma told be she already knew about the doll and Millie's mother was going to invite me to tea to make her acquaintance, the very day Millie received her.

When, at last, the invitation arrived, I could hardly wait for tea-time. Mamma let me wear my very best frock but as Molly had no gown befitting the occasion, Mamma suggested I should leave her at home. I agreed to this readily enough, having become aware of her hairlessness and fearing this might be more noticeable were she to be seated beside the French doll whose ringlets, in my imagination, had by this time assumed a tremendous thickness and length.

Millie was waiting for me at the gate. She had a paper bag in her hand. "Look!" she greeted me, "Mamma has given us some biscuits. We can play picnics."

"But your doll," I said, "your new doll! Aren't you going to show her to me?"

"Not out here," said Millie. "Wait until we go in. You'll see her then."

I had to bide my time in patience but when, at last, we were called in, there was still no sign of the French doll. It wasn't until we had finished our tea that Millie's mother said, "Now Millie, you may show Cathy your doll, but be careful!".

Millie went behind the sofa and dragged out a large box. She took off the lid and proceeded to remove layers of white tissue paper. At last, the French doll from Paris lay revealed in all her beauty. I gasped. Never had I seen so gorgeous a doll. She was dressed entirely in a delicate shade of pink, her big brown eyes shone like stars and all around her smiling face and falling over her shoulders, were the golden curls that I had dreamed of. "Oh," I breathed, stretching out my arms, "may I lift her up?".

"No, no," cried Millie, "Mamma says we mustn't take her out of the box." "But", she added appeasingly, "when Mamma comes back, I'll ask her to pull the string and you'll hear her say 'Ma-ma".'

That didn't impress me. "Let's comb her hair," I suggested. We needn't lift her out of the box." Millie was horrified. "We mustn't touch her curls," she said. "They have to be combed in a special way. She's a French doll, remember."

That was too much. My disappointment was so great I could hardly keep back the tears. All I wanted now was to get home. I told Millie it was time for me to go and, without waiting to say "thank you" to her mother, I left the house and ran home. There, I rushed into my mother's arms and wept uncontrollably. "We couldn't play with her," I sobbed. "Millie wouldn't let me touch her."

"I thought that might be the way," said Mother, "but never mind, come upstairs, there's a surprise waiting for you." We went upstairs to my bedroom and there, sitting on a chair, was a doll with long golden curls! At first, I thought it was a new doll, even a French doll from Paris, but when I looked closer, I saw that it was none other than my own dear Molly.

"Well," smiled Mamma, "do you like her?"

"What happened?" I stammered.

"I took her to the Dolls' Hospital while you were at Millie's," said Mother, "and had her fitted with a wig. You can brush it and comb it as much as you like, it's real hair."

I took dear Molly in my arms and I think at that moment I must have been the happiest child in the whole world.

TWO BIRTHDAYS — TWO DOLLS

We were a poor family, but Mother's superior ways had won us some esteem in our village. She had been a nurse maid in a County family and had learnt good manners and how to speak nicely. She brought her children up in the same way, and I think it must have been on account of this that I used to be invited to go and play with Mary, the little girl up at the 'Big House' who was an only child and very lonely.

I was a year older than Mary but strangely enough, our birthdays were on the same day. We were very good friends and always enjoyed the time we spent together. We usually played in Mary's nursery where there were shelves littered with toys. She never gave me anything, nor indeed did I expect it for we were brought up in the belief that God had made us high and lowly and by that we must abide. At other times, we played in the garden and sometimes, as a treat, we were allowed to walk out together as far as the toy shop in the village. We didn't go into the shop, we just stood gazing at the motley collection of lucky bags, dolls, paint boxes, picture books, shuttlecocks, tops and marbles piled in the window. Everything was of the cheapest to suit the pockets of the village children. But on one never-to-be forgotten occasion, propped up against the back of the window, was a china doll costing the unheard of sum of two shillings. It was a pretty little doll dressed in flowered muslin and Mary was greatly taken with it. She talked of nothing else all the way back.

When I got home, I told Mother about the little doll. "I wish we were rich," I said, "then I could buy that doll for Mary's birthday."

Mother, used to solving problems, suggested I might manage to save up two shillings by doing jobs for people. "After all," she said, "it isn't Mary's birthday for quite a long time".

I thought this was a very good idea and I set to work with a will, cleaning steps, collecting sticks, running messages and even selling little cakes from door to door that Mother made. Every day I visited the toy shop to make sure no-one had bought the doll and every day I pictured Mary's pleasure and surprise when she received it.

At last, the day before Mary's birthday — which was also mine, I had collected one shilling and ninepence, and poor Mother sacrificed three pennies to make up the two shillings. Greatly excited, I went off to make my purchase. Mr. Blythe of the toy shop, was surprised when I asked for the doll. He was a kindly man used to dealing with children's limited means. He evidently thought I had mistaken the price of the doll and not wishing to embarrass me, he produced another doll exactly the same except that it was disfigured by a crack across its forhead. "Now," he said in his accommodating way, "that doll in the window is two shillings but this one is only sixpence. If you make it a little bonnet, no-one will see the crack."

As if I would give Mary a cracked doll! The idea appalled me. "I want the doll in the window," I said, putting my money down on the counter. Realizing I was in earnest Mr. Blythe wrapped up the doll and gave it to me.

I couldn't sleep that night, thinking of the wonderful surprise I was about to give Mary, and early in the morning, I hurried up to the 'Big House' with my precious parcel. I left it with one of the servants with the message Mother had instilled into me — "Please will you give this to Miss Mary from Jessie."

My mission accomplished, I skipped with joy all the way home. When I got there, to my astonishment, I found a parcel waiting for me! "It's from Mary," Mother explained.

Trembling with excitement, I unwrapped the parcel. And what did I find inside? The cracked doll!

A DRESS FOR BEATRICE

When I was seven years old, Mother made me a lovely cotton frock for my birthday. It wasn't a surprise, I had chosen the cloth myself. It was pale green with dark green grasses, and buttercups and daisies all over it. The girl in the shop said the design represented a meadow and that was why I had chosen it, it seemed just right for summer. I had chosen the pattern for the frock too. It was in a big envelope with a picture on the front of a little girl wearing the frock. I noticed it had two pockets and that was why I had chosen that particular pattern. I was very fond of pockets!

The finished frock was beautiful. I ran upstairs forthwith and put it on, then I pirouetted round the house in it, finally coming to rest in the sitting-room where Beatrice, my doll, was sitting. "Do you like my new frock, Beatrice?" I asked.

Beatrice, of course, made no reply but Mother was quick to see in my remark an opening for introducing me to the delights of dress-making. "Why don't you make Beatrice a new dress too?" she said. "There are plenty of bits left over from yours."

I fell straight into the trap. The idea excited me and I was anxious to start right away. Mother, needless to say, was delighted, for she usually had great difficulty in persuading me to take up a needle. "I'll help you," she said encouragingly.

"Oh, no" I said. "I'm going to make it myself."

Mother must have been a little dubious, but she gave me the bits, and some lace and ribbons too, and I set to work. I spent several days making the frock, taking the very smallest stitches and decorating it with a vulgar abundance of lace. The finished confection I considered beyond compare and, bursting with pride, I showed it to Mother. "Look, Mamma!" I said. Beatrice's frock!".

Mother took the frock in her hands and looked at it for a long time. "But ..." she wavered at length, "it's too small. It wouldn't go on to Beatrice."

I stared at it aghast. Compared with Beatrice's buxom figure, it certainly was minute, but anything so mundane as size had never crossed my mind. I burst into tears. Mother tried to comfort me but what she said or what we did, I do not remember. All I remember was the horrifying realization that a frock, unless it fitted, was useless.

A PATHETIC STORY

I began to study music before I was four years old and I was obliged to give up so much time to it, there was none left for playthings. My harp and my piano were my dolls, and actually, I never possessed a real one all my life. I believe they are most interesting creatures to most little girls, but I was never able to study them.

Madame Albani.
(A famous singer)

A PRESENT FROM MY SWEETHEART

The doll I loved best when I was young was really not a doll at all but an ornament. It was made of highly glazed china and represented a little girl in cloak and bonnet. This treasure was given to me by my sweetheart when I was four years old.

It was at this age I started school. The local Elementary School had only just been opened and it was the pride of the town. I was put in the 'Baby Room'. This, with its tables and chairs instead of the customary desks with turn-up seats, its rocking-boat and sand-pit, its 'occupations' was considered the last word in modernity. But despite all these innovations, instruction still came first and we spent the mornings chanting lists of words from the blackboard m-a-t mat, c-a-t cat, b-a-t bat, droning our times-tables and tracing letters and figures in sand. If there chanced to be a little time left over at the end of the morning, we were 'treated' to the rabbit.

The rabbit was a small furry object with a key to wind it up. For the 'treat', we sat in a semi-circle in front of the teacher who, when everyone was sitting rigidly straight with hands on knees, wound up the rabbit and set it down on the floor. It then jumped across the floor and whichever child it happened to reach was required to lift it up and reverse it, so that it jumped back to the teacher. Every now and again some unfortunate child did it wrong and instead of jumping back after the desired fashion, the wretched rabbit lurched over on its side and lay there buzzing frantically to no effect until the teacher, after duly reprimanding the culprit, plunged forward and re-erected it.

We were treated to the rabbit on my first morning in school, and I sat frozen to my chair in fear of incurring the teacher's wrath, should I be the one to do it wrong. "Oh God," I prayed urgently and silently in familiar phrases, "let not this rabbit come near me. In Thy mercy, let it not, I beseech Thee."

But God did not see fit to comply and soon, to my horror, I saw the rabbit making a bee-line for me. So intense was my fear that the child sitting next to me must have felt it, and as the rabbit approached the leg of my chair, a little hand grabbed it and deftly reversed it. I was saved! I turned to my rescuer and found he was a little black boy. We stared at one another in mute understanding, and from that moment, we were sweethearts.

In the afternoons we had 'occupations' and sometimes singing or dancing. Occupations consisted chiefly of bead-threading and lacing, but before we could thread the huge wooden beads or lace up the flapping pieces of leather meant to represent the fronts of boots, we had to acquire a lace from a great tangled bundle of these. Everyone tugged and pulled until by some lucky chance they managed to free one, but I never had to join in the fray for my little sweetheart always came to my aid. With expert skill he would extract a lace and smilingly present me with it.

Dancing, which we had in the hall, a vast empty space surrounded by class-rooms, was the one lesson I liked. To start with we all had to find a partner and I need not say who always found me! The dances we learnt were Country Dances with delightful names where boys and girls faced one another in long lines, advancing to meet, turning one another round and galloping round the room holding hands. It was all hilarious fun because the teacher occupied at the keyboard, could not keep her eye on us. Had this not been the case, she might have witnessed the transference of the little china ornament from my partner to myself during 'Haste to the Wedding'! It was when we advanced to meet that he took the opportunity of pressing it into my hand. At first I thought if was a bottle of perfume because of its strong scent of violets, but a brief glance showed me what it was and I pushed it into my pocket with my handkerchief on top to keep it safe, and went on dancing.

The rest of the afternoon I was in a state of suppressed excitement, thinking of the treasure hiding in my pocket, for in those days we possessed little, and anything, a glass bead, a pretty button, a piece of ribbon, was precious. I had to wait until I got home to look at it properly, and when I did, I was completely charmed by it. It was the figure of a little girl with a smiling face, dressed in a bright blue bonnet and cloak. The figure was hollow, and from the hollow depths came the mysterious scent of violets. It was magic! I ran to show it to my mother. "Who gave it to you?" she asked.

"A little boy in school," I replied.

Mother seemed a little concerned. "But are you sure you should have taken it?" she persisted.

"Oh, yes," I said. "I didn't ask for it."

That seemed to satisfy her and she said no more except to caution me to put it away somewhere before I fell with it and cut myself. So I carried the precious little girl upstairs and put her on the mantlepiece beside my bed. I named her 'Violet' because of her scent, and that night and every night, I took her into bed with me and talked to her. I felt that she expected me to do this and that in return she would preserve me from the perils of the night. Violet had become my talisman!

I had Violet for years. Even when I was quite old, she remained in her place on my mantelpiece. Her appearance may have been garish and her scent sickly, but I loved her. What become of her in the end I do not know but I shall never forget her, just as I shall never forget the little sweetheart who gave her to me nearly eighty years ago.

Girl and doll — always an appealing subject

A more roguish study

THE DANCING DOLLS

When I was eight years old I nearly died of pneumonia. I remember being in such pain I wished I could die. However, my mother, after waiting in vain for the Doctor to come, took matters into her own hands and applied a bread poultice. This saved my life.

For some time after this I was very weak and took no interest in anything. Poor Mother was in despair. She used to bring me little novelties when she went shopping and although I was pleased, I didn't play with them. My sister used to read to me but I didn't listen. It was my brother Archie who eventually roused me from my apathy with his little dancing dolls. Archie was considerably older than my sister and me and, unlike most brothers, was always kind to his two little sisters. He wanted me to get better, and put himself out to speed my recovery.

Archie found the pattern for the little dolls in 'The Boys' Own Paper'. They were cardboard figures with the limbs loosely attached to the body with paper fasteners. By pulling a dangling string attached to a combination of strings behind, the figure could be made to perform all kinds of antics, and when accompanied by words and song, they were laughable indeed.

One morning, I heard a merry whistling outside my half-open door and in a minute, a funny little cardboard doll came round the door, dancing up and down in a frantic fashion. It began to address remarks to me in a squeaky little voice — "How are you to-day?" "Are you feeling better?" "Are you getting up soon?" Then Archie came in and presented me with this little wonder, telling me that he had made it specially for me. I was charmed. He pinned it to the mantlepiece beside my bed so that I could make it dance whenever I liked. "His name is 'Percy'," he said. "'P' is the first letter in 'Pneumonia', and if you think of names for the other letters, I'll make you the dolls. There's room for them all on the mantlepiece."

Archie gave me the word 'PNEUMONIA' printed on a piece of paper to help me and I had no difficulty in finding names, I just thought of the children in school amongst whom there was even a 'Una' for 'U'. After this, I made a rapid recovery. I forgot I was ill because my mind was completely occupied with the little dancing dolls. When the 'set' was finished, we played games with the dolls. 'School' was a favourite, we jerked them about as they answered our questions in funny little voices. We let them converse with one another, sing songs, recite poems, play out stories. There was no end to the games we invented. Long after I was well again, we still played with the little dolls and when eventually, we lost interest in them, they were not destroyed but packed away in a box labelled 'PNEUMONIA'.

MISUNDERSTOOD

When I was a little girl I had more than my share of dolls because my sister Margery, three years older than myself, always gave me hers, for she didn't care for dolls at all. Our dolls came from a rich aunt who delighted in sending us presents. She christened the dolls herself, and they would arrive with the names of her choice neatly printed on little cards tied round their wrists. The dolls were pretty and went to sleep, but their names were not pretty at all — 'Ada' 'Ivy' 'Sarah' 'Jane; even 'Maude'. I think it was on account of the austerity of their names that I never felt any affection for these dolls. Certainly, I played with them, my favourite game being 'Hospitals' because, with their sleeping eyes, they died so nicely, but somehow, they always remained aloof.

"I wish I could have a doll from a shop" I confided in Margery one day, "I would call her 'Kitty' ". 'Kitty' seemed to be a name of exquisite charm.

"Perhaps Mamma would let you use your money-box money to buy one," suggested Margery, after due consideration.

I didn't think this was very likely, but I thought I would see, so I ran into the kitchen where Mother was busy baking, and said, "Mamma, may I buy a doll with the money in my money box?"

"Yes," she murmured without looking up.

Here, I must explain that our poor mother had far too much to do. There were four of us children for there were twin boys older than Margery, and Father's salary as a journalist, did not stretch to providing any help in the house. Consequently, her mind on two or three things at once, Mother would often accede to our requests without being really aware of what they were. This must have been the case when I asked about my money-box for I well remember how annoyed she was when, a little later, she discovered us coaxing the coins out on a knife.

However, all must have ended amicably for, later on, Margery accompanied me to the toy shop to make my purchase. I had no difficulty in choosing a doll because 'Kitty' was sitting on a shelf waiting for me. I had never seen her before but I recognized her at once as the doll of my dreams. She looked younger than any of my dolls at home, she had dimples in her cheeks and her tongue was plainly visible inside her mouth, a feature I thought especially attractive. I do not remember how much we paid for the doll but I know we had sixpence over which we spent on chocolates, and that was an unforgettable treat.

'Kitty' was a great success. Even Margery took a little interest in her, advising me not to do her hair too much and then it would stay nice and curly instead of turning into the usual matted mass. And Mother did something quite astounding, she made a nightdress for Kitty! This was the only article of doll's clothing I ever remember her making. As for me, I loved Kitty so much and became so wrapped up in her, I began to imagine she was alive. I knew she wasn't, but I treated her as if she were. She became as it were, a 'living' doll to me.

When I had had Kitty for about a year, I was seven and it was time to start school. I was all eagerness to start but Mother upset me by telling me how lonely she would be when I was gone. "I shall have no-one to talk to all day long," she said.

Poor Mamma! I pictured her in the empty house crying because she was so lonely. The picture made me want to cry myself. But just in time, I had a brilliant idea. Mamma could have Kitty to play with! I knew that being grown up, she wouldn't want anyone to see her playing with a doll, but there would be no-one to see her so she could enjoy herself to her heart's content.

School proved highly agreeable and my mind was at rest about Mamma. There was no possibility of her being lonely for, every day before I left, I took care to place Kitty in a conspicuous position in the sitting room where she would find her and play with her. Sometimes, I would put a little pile of clothes beside her so that Mamma could enjoy changing her outfits, or a sponge that she might wash her face, or a ribbon to tie in her hair. There was no doubt in my mind that Mamma really did play with Kitty because everything was arranged differently when I got home. My secret made me very happy and strengthened the bond between Kitty and myself.

But alas, there came a day when I overdid things. I thought Mamma would enjoy having a tea-party, so I left my dolls' tea-set out with Kitty, and a little bag of sugared biscuits I had saved. When I got home, Mamma was cross. "I wish, Lizzie," she said, "you wouldn't leave all your things lying about when you go to school. And put your doll away in the future, I'm tired of having to avoid knocking it over."

These sharp words stunned me. Never for a moment had I imagined that Mamma's feelings towards Kitty were any different from my own. Now I was faced by the startling revelation that she regarded my beloved doll only as a 'thing' that was in the way. Poor Kitty! Poor me! How deluded we had been! But we had learnt our lesson and never again would we be so foolish as to invite a grown-up to share our intimate little world.

Comforting the needy

AN UNWANTED GIFT

Most people had a maid when I was young but we couldn't afford one. We had to manage with 'Hannah,' a woman who came once a week to do the rough work. This consisted of cleaning the steps, scrubbing the floors, black-leading the grates, polishing the brasses, breaking coal and chopping up sticks. Poor Hannah! Hard work had made her old before her time. With her chalky face, frizzy hair and string of jet beads around her throat, she seemed to be immensely old. And yet I know she was young because at one time, she used to bring 'Katie,' her two-year-old daughter with her when she came to work, having no-one to leave her with. It is Katie, or rather Katie and her doll, that this story is about.

Katie was a poor little thing with very thin legs weighed down by heavy boots. Her clothing was made up of odds and ends, and merging into these and always in her arms, was a bundle of rags and towelling. This was her 'doll' her support and comforter. I wouldn't have known the bundle was a doll if Mother hadn't told me, explaining that poor people like Hannah had no money to buy a proper doll. It seemed very sad to me.

When Hannah came to work, she would carry Katie into the kitchen and put her down in a little wicker arm-chair, and there she would remain all day nursing her 'baby,' never making a sound, never crying, never laughing. At first, I tried to play with her, but it was no use, she resisted all my overtures. At last, one day, I decided that poor little Katie must be very unhappy. The best way to remedy this, I thought, would be to give her a proper doll. With this in view, I took out all my dolls and studied them. I loved them all and didn't want to part with any, but I really was anxious to

35

make Katie happy, so, after lengthy consideration, I decided to give her a small wax doll dressed in baby clothes, as this seemed in size and dress to be the most appropriate.

In happy anticipation of the pleasure I was about to give Katie, I ran off to the kitchen with the little doll. "Here you are, Katie," I said, holding it out to her.

There was no response. "Take it," I urged, "it's for you."

Still there was no response. So, in desperation, I tried to pull the rag doll from her that I might replace it with the 'proper' doll. Never shall I forget the result of my action. The expressionless face became contorted, and the silent child emitted a piercing scream that brought Hannah rushing to the kitchen. Hannah picked up Katie and soothed her, and Mother said to me, "What happened? What did you do to her?"

"I tried to give her my doll," I said.

"Katie's got a doll," said Hannah.

Mother led me from the kitchen, explaining that Katie was used to her rag doll and didn't want another. But how could she possibly prefer a bundle of old rags to my beautiful wax baby, I wondered. And the more I wondered, the more incredible it seemed. Little did I know how near to shattering her little world, I had been.

PEG DOLLS

I started school early so I was put in the 'Baby Room' until I reached the advanced age of five. During my time there, I remember, very clearly, three deaths amongst my companions. The first was one of twins. The twins, a boy and a girl, occupied a table next to the one I shared with a little girl called Rosie. They both had enormous brown eyes, they never spoke and never let go one another's hands. After a time, they were missing and their little chairs remained empty for a long time. Then, one day, the little boy came back alone and I heard from the other children that his sister had died of diphtheria. I remember seeing the little boy wandering about the playground all by himself, his arms hanging loosely by his sides, and I felt sorry for him.

The second death was that of a boy called Wilfred. Wilfred's appearance was startling. His face was of a deadly pallor and his hair so thin and light in colour as to be invisible. He was, I remember, always begging for sweets, if he saw children with any, he would advance towards them with hand outstretched, his very looks commanding compliance. Poor Wilfred. One day, his mother came to school to say that he had been taken to hospital. Some time later, she came again and this time she had her husband with her. Miss Barnes, our teacher, held a whispered conversation with them, and finally, took down a crayoned drawing from the wall which she gave to them. They looked at it and then went away. But no sooner had the door closed on them than a boy called Tom stood up and said, "Please, Miss Barnes, that was my drawing they took."

Miss Barnes was taken aback for she had obviously thought the drawing was Wilfred's. However, she quickly recovered and said, "Well, Tom, surely you don't grudge it to them when poor Wilfred is dead."

At this, Tom, in his turn, was taken aback and sat down without further demur.

The third death I remember only too well. It was of Rosie, the little girl who shared my table. She was a chubby little girl with curly hair. She was always laughing and when she laughed, her curls seemed to tumble about. One day, Miss Barnes told us we were going to make 'peg dolls' the following day. "I'll give you the pegs," she said, "but you must all bring some pretty bits to dress them in."

"I can't," whispered Rosie to me with a shake of her curls. "My Mammy hasn't got any bits."

When I got home I told my mother about Miss Barnes's request and she sent me to our dress-maker who gave me a bundle of beautiful bits. I remember particularly some pieces of brightly coloured ribbon of appreciable length. I was excited and delighted with my hoard and could not get to school quick enough with it.

When the time came for making the peg dolls, Miss Barnes asked us to put our bits out on our tables and she would come round and look at what we had brought. When I opened my bundle, ribbons, lace, silks and satins cascaded all over the table but I instantly swept them into a heap in front of me. Poor little Rosie who had brought nothing, laughed with delight at the sight of my glorious bits and could not refrain from extending a chubby little hand to touch them, but every time she did so, I pushed her hand away. When Miss Barnes reached our table, she said, noticing the empty space in front of Rosie, "Haven't you brought anything Rosie? Well, never mind, Janie (that was me) will share hers with you."

"Oh, no I won't," I shouted. "They're mine!".

Miss Barnes surveyed me with horror. "I'm surprised at you," she said. "Your mother would want you to share them, I'm sure."

"No, she wouldn't," I cried. And on that rebellious note, my memory of the incident ends. No doubt, the vehemence of my feelings obliterated everything else. I must add that ever since I have been ashamed to think I was capable of such outrageous behaviour.

Soon after the episode of the peg dolls, Rosie was away from school and Miss Barnes ushered a new girl into her chair, explaining to me that Rosie was ill with pneumonia and would not be back for a long time. The new girl's name was Hazel and she was just the opposite to Rosie with short straight hair cut in a fringe and very thin arms and legs. We liked one another at once and soon became close friends. I'm afraid I forgot all about Rosie until one morning I heard the children whispering to one another that Rosie was dead. Then, one boy, determined to have the news from an authoratative source, addressed Miss Barnes by saying, "Please, Miss Barnes, is it true that Rosie Roberts is going down a bury-hole?"

Miss Barnes paused for a moment before replying, probably shocked by this horrific mode of expression. "Rosie has gone to Heaven," she said at last.

"I'm glad," said a little girl called Connie, possibly trying to hide her real feelings of grief.

As for me, I was not haunted by Rosie's death as I might well have been. Hazel's friendship had softened the blow for me. Nevertheless, all through my life I wished I had not so cruelly deprived the poor little girl of a share of my largesse on that day we made peg dolls in the Baby Room.

Preparing for Sunday
'Haste ! put your play-things all away,
Tomorrow is the Sabbath-day'

40

REMEMBER THE SABBATH DAY
TO KEEP IT HOLY

Marmalade and my father's Adam's Apple are the two things I associate with Sunday long ago. The first, because we had bread and marmalade for breakfeast instead of the usual porridge; the second, because afterwards, when we knelt cosily together to listen to Father addressing the Almighty, I kept my eyes open to enjoy the spectacle of his very prominent Adam's Apple emphasizing the fervour of his entreaties.

I hated Sunday as I am sure the others did too. It was heralded in on Saturday night for my sister Ruthie and me, by the relegation of our dear familiar dolls and toys to the playroom, there to remain until Monday. Father who was usually cross, seemed crosser than ever on Sunday. The slightest little thing such as leaving a small crust on our plates or speaking out of turn, would upset him and lead to a dreadful scene. After our marmalade breakfast and prayers, we all proceeded to church — with our collection. Being the youngest, I only had a penny, and the dropping of that penny into the collection bag was nothing short of a nightmare to me because once, I hadn't aimed quite straight, and it had landed on the floor and rolled away down the aisle, causing a stir of suppressed mirth which reduced me to a state of nothingness. The church service seemed interminable, and the pressure of my Sunday hat on my Sunday bow of hair ribbon was agony in the extreme.

On our return from church, we had a dinner of bread and cold mutton because our parents considered it wrong to cook on Sunday. The practically raw red meat disgusted me and I always cut my piece into dice which I swallowed whole so that I couldn't taste them. After dinner, we gathered for 'Bible Study' when we read a chapter taking the verses turn about. Father expounded on the verses as we went along, asking us a great many questions and expecting us, in our turn, to ask him questions. I never dared voice the only question I longed to ask and that was, "If God was God, couldn't He have had a lot of Sons?" Later in the afternoon, we went for a walk in Noah's Ark fashion, two by two - two girls, two boys, two parents. After tea, we looked at Sunday books until bed-time. We never had supper on Sunday in order to give Mother a rest.

41

You may imagine our jubilation when, one Sunday, we learned that this tedious routine was to be broken. Mother and Father were going to a special service in the evening and we children were to be left alone in the house. During our walk, Ruthie and I discussed what we would do 'while the cat was away', Let's ask Bobbie to make us some packets for our shop, suggested Ruthie at length.

"Oh, yes," I agreed. "Mrs. Machin's cupboard is empty."

'Mrs. Machin' was the mother of the family in our Dolls' house. Our shop was only a collection of small tins and boxes but we had delightful times with it. One of us would be the shop-keeper, and the other would take Mrs. Machin to make her purchases, speaking for her in a funny little voice.

As soon as we had the opportunity, we put the question to our brother Bobbie. He agreed readily enough, for not only was he a good-natured boy but he enjoyed making the packets which were tiny folds of paper containing sugar, tea, cocoa, rice - anything that we could take from the kitchen without it being noticed. He would label the packets in minute printing and decorate them with flowers and scrolls in bright colours from his paint box. Each was a little work of art.

After tea, we thought Mother and Father would never go but, at last, after giving us many instructions as to what we were not to do, they left. Edward our eldest brother, who was far too old to play, immediately disappeared to his room with his books, and Bobbie, Ruthie and I hastened to the forbidden play-room. When Bobbie was nicely started on the packets, Ruthie and I repaired to the kitchen to raid the cupboard for supplies. When we returned to the playroom the table was gay with coloured packets waiting to be filled. What fun we had putting in pinches of the various items we had collected!

So engrossed were we in our work, we entirely forgot the time and imagine our horror when we heard the front door opening! Our parents had returned! There was no time to put anything away. We just shut the play-room door and went downstairs. But the evidence of our crime was stamped on each one of us. Bobbie's fingers were thick with paint and Ruthie's and mine were almost as bad. Father met us at the foot of the stairs and manouvred us up again. He opened the play-room door and glancing at the littered table, told us we had broken the Fourth Commandment, disobeyed God and put our very souls in jeopardy. Our precious packets were consigned to the kitchen fire, we were ordered to bed and poor little Bobbie warned that he would be 'dealt with' in the morning.

Later on, when we were discussing the incident, Bobbie observed, "One of us should have kept cavee."

Ruthie and I agreed wholeheartedly, we would know better another time. Father had taught us a lesson but hardly the one he had intended.

THE TEA-PARTY

We were having a tea-party, Mamma and I, at least we were having two tea-parties, mine was in the nursery and Mamma's in the drawing room. I was having two guests, my friend Barbara and her doll Agatha, but Mamma was having only one, Barbara's mother.

I had wanted to have a dolls' tea-party ever since I had visited my cousins and found them having one. I had experienced the most delightful grown-up feeling as I sat sipping tea with them from their dolls' tea cups and chatting about our 'children'. I thought it would feel even better if I were to be the hostess, so, when Mamma told me that she had invited Barbara and her mother to tea, I asked her if I might have a dolls' tea-party with Barbara. She agreed but said I must do things correctly.

Mamma provided a lace tray-cloth and we spread it on my own small table which was a comfortable size for two children and two dolls. We then laid the table with my 'Maiden Hair' tea-set which was so precious it had to be kept in its own wooden box. Secretly, I disliked this tea-set on account of its having been handled by the dead. It had been bequeathed to me by an old lady and presented to me with the simple explanation that it was a present from 'Old Mrs Wright'. Knowing her to be dead, I quite naturally assumed she had wrapped up the box in Heaven and posted it in some ethereal post office. However, I did not let my private qualms spoil the tea-party and joyfully accepted the tiny biscuits with stars of sugar on the top, and the minute pieces of bread and butter Mamma gave me to fill the two cake plates. We put milk for 'tea' in the tea-pot and real lumps of sugar in the sugar basin which had a little tongs for lifting them out. "There," said Mamma, "your tea-party's ready. Don't forget to ask Barbara if she takes sugar and cream, and don't forget to pass her the plates before taking anything yourself. Remember, you are the hostess."

"Yes, Mamma," I said, little dreaming that I would be the worst hostess that ever was.

A little later, when 'Marian', my best china doll, decked out in her best muslin frock, was seated in readiness at the tea table, we set out to call for Barbara and her mother as this was the arrangement we had made. As we walked along, Mamma said, "I shouldn't tell Barbara about the tea-party. Let it be a surprise for her."

I had forgotten about Barbara but these words brought her back to mind. I had never liked her. She was a sickly child who always had to have her own way and the best of everything, or she cried. I knew the reason she was so spoiled was because she was so often ill and had been at Death's door more than once, but I felt no compassion for her, and if Mamma had known the evil thoughts that were surging in my mind as we walked along together, I am sure she would have felt like disowning me. I KNEW what Barbara would do as soon as she saw my tea-party. She would grab my little sugar biscuits and gobble them up one after another. Why had I not thought of hiding some, or ALL of them! By the time we reached Barbara's house, I had begun to wish most fervently that we might find her stricken with some fell disease or even dead. But no, nothing so accommodating had happened. There was Barbara, apparently in the best of health, dressed in her Sunday clothes, with 'Agatha', her doll, cradled on her arm and a 'Dorothy' bag hanging from her wrist.

As we walked home together in front of our two Mammas, Barbara said, "I know we are having a dolls' tea-party."

"Who told you?" I demanded.

"Mamma," said Barbara. "Your Mamma told her."

That was the end. Barbara had been prepared and my biscuits were doomed. The imminence of their fate stirred my mind into action and, by the time we drew near our gate, I had worked out a plan to prevent greedy Barbara from having a single one of my little sugar biscuits.

"Would you like to look at the garden before we go in?" said my Mamma to Barbara's as we all hovered near the front door.

Barbara's mother agreed politely and they all moved across the grass together. Everything was happening just as I had expected, for all our visitors were subjected to a tour of the garden before going into the house. I hung behind and as soon as they were safely on their way I pushed open the front door and dashed upstairs to the nursery. Once there, I stood before the beautifully arranged tea table where Maria was still patiently waiting, and began thrusting the little biscuits into my mouth with horrifying speed. I nearly choked but what did it matter, my end was accomplished.

Breathlessly, I hurried downstairs again and joined the others in the garden. We all went into the house then, and up to the nursery. Barbara and I went in but our mothers stood in the doorway admiring the scene, but only for a moment for which I was thankful, or Mamma might have noticed the absence of the biscuits. As they turned away, Barbara's mother called out, "Don't forget what's in your bag, Barbara."

At that, Barbara seated Agatha in a chair, then, drawing open the strings of the 'Dorothy' bag, she produced a 'poke' bag filled with little sugar biscuits exactly the same as the ones I had so greedily disposed of only a few moments before. Words cannot describe my shame. I had felt guilty enough when I joined the others in the garden, but now.....! I never told anyone of my dastardly deed, but the memory of it has remained with me all my life and I am ashamed to think what a truly horrible child I must have been.

46

THE NEW HEAD

Some dolls are life-long treasures. Madeleine is one of these and what a beautiful doll she is with her rosy cheeks and dimpled chin, her pearly teeth and shining eyes, not to mention her luxuriant chestnut hair. Who would believe that she is seventy-five years old! She must have looked much the same on that Christmas morning long ago when her 'Mamma,' then only four and a half years old, woke to find her sitting at the foot of her bed.

Yes, Madeleine was my Christmas present in 1896, but I was acquainted with her before this. For weeks she had been sitting in the toyshop window and every time we went down town I would say to Mother, "May we go and look in the toyshop, Mamma? Please!" And there I would stand in front of the window, transfixed by the sight of this wonderful doll. It wasn't her dress that attracted me, indeed, she only wore a little white chemise; it wasn't her smiling face, although that left nothing to be desired, it was her hair! It wasn't the usual curly kind, it was thick and straight and hung down to her waist. I had never seen such hair and every time I looked at it, I marvelled at it more.

But a dreadful shock was in store for me. One day when I looked in at the window, the doll had vanished! In her place was an empty space. "Where is she, Mamma?" I said in a very small voice.

My mother merely took my hand and as she led me away, said casually, "Somebody must have bought her, I suppose."

This eventuality had never entered my head. I was heart-broken. Little did I know that it was my own mother who had bought the doll! You may imagine my utter astonishment and joy when I woke on Christmas morning to find her sitting before me on the bed. She was fully dressed now and wore a tailored coat and smart little hat exactly like my own. But I recognized her immediately because, beneath that smart little hat, her chestnut hair hung down to her waist. Was she really for me, I wondered. I couldn't believe it. But Mother came into my room then and put an end to my doubts. "Well," she said, "Do you like your doll? She is a present from Father and me."

There was no nonsense about Father Christmas because my parents thought it wrong to tell children untruths. But oh, how I envied children who could hang up their stockings for that jolly old man to fill, and how I longed for a Christmas tree with a fairy on the top, another delight that was taboo.

I called my doll 'Madeleine' because that was the longest and loveliest name I could think of. I needn't say that at the first opportunity I tried combing Madeleine's hair, and the very act of combing it roused by maternal instincts and I felt I really was her mother.

One day, a great tragedy occurred. I was carrying Madeleine round the garden when I slipped and fell. Poor Madeleine fell too and when I picked her up, to my horror, I saw a large crack across her forehead. I carried her into the house, crying bitterly. Mother took her from me and said, "She'll have to go the Doll's Hospital."

I knew all about hospitals for on several occasions I had visited the Children's Hospital with my mother. Naturally, I based my idea of a Dolls' Hospital on this. There would be rows of little beds with dolls in them, I thought, and kind nurses with bowls in their hands. I was quite sure Madeleine would be happy in hospital.

When Madeleine came home again, Mother handed her to me and said, "Here you are, your doll has come back."

Madeleine's crack had completely disappeared. What a marvellous recovery she had made! "What did they do to her?" I asked, expecting to be told about bandages and dressings.

"Oh," said Mother, "they gave her a new head, I suppose."

I must have looked askance for she added by way of explanation, "They always keep a supply of spare heads".

I looked at Madeleine lying in my arms. The familiar face smiled up at me, the familiar hair hung round her. A new head! How could Mamma be so mistaken! I felt quite sorry for her.

Madeleine never had another accident and we were never parted again. And although I look old and she looks young, I assure you there is very little difference in our ages."

Madeleine of the Chestnut Hair
The New Head

EMILY'S RETURN

We were a large family and very poor. I never remember my mother doing anything but work, and I hardly ever saw my father, he went to work so early and came home again so late. I was the youngest, at least for a long time, and my sister Emily, eight years older, took complete charge of me. There were some boys in between but they took care of themselves. I often wished I were not the baby, I thought it would be nice to be like Emily and have a little sister to do my bidding.

One summer's day, Emily told me she had a great treat in store for me. That afternoon she was going to take me to the Fair in Barlow, a neighbouring village some three miles away. I was greatly excited for I was familiar with fairs and all their fascinations for they were the highlights of the year in every village. There would be stalls full of toys and trinkets, merry-go-rounds, Punch and Judy shows, coconut shies, coloured sweets, lemonade, and tinkling music. Emily warned me that I mustn't be asking for rides and refreshments because she had no money for these, but she needn't have worried, for, when she bought me a little doll dressed in pink paper I was so happy I didn't want anything else. We just wandered about and enjoyed watching others enjoying themselves.

When we got home, I was very tired for, of course we had had to walk each way, and I think I was only about six at the time. Emily put me straight to bed. She kissed me goodnight and promised to make me a proper dress for the little doll the very next day. I asked if it could have some lace on it and she smiled and said "Yes". But the little pink doll was never dressed, neither did I ever see Emily's smiling face again for, that night, she died. What she died of I was never told, apparently, she just died in her sleep. "God had need of her in Heaven," said my father, and that was all the explanation I was given.

I was shocked and confused and could not understand my feelings, but the full horror of the event did not dawn on me until I saw Emily's coffin being lowered into the grave. Even then, I was not as much concerned with Emily as I was with myself. Could this happen to me, I wondered. Could God suddenly have need of me in Heaven? The thought of being put into a deep, black hole terrified me. I hid my little doll away at the back of a drawer trying, I suppose, to hide away the horror it represented. Every night became a nightmare to me. I lay in bed forcing myself to stay awake, lest, if I went to sleep I might never wake. How very miserable I was! By day, I had no kind Emily to take care of me, and by night, I was beset by fears. No-one knew of my sufferings, no-one took any notice of me. In time, however, something happened which put an end to my miseries.

"Come and see," said my father, one morning, "You have a baby sister."

Greatly wondering, I followed him into the bedroom where my mother lay in bed, with a tiny baby no bigger than a doll beside her. "It's Emily," she said.

My parents, following a common practice at that time, had decided to give the new baby her dead sister's name. But I knew nothing of this, I didn't even know that babies were born, I thought a mother woke up to find one lying beside her in bed — a little surprise from God! So I accepted the return of Emily as a new-born baby as just another variety of God's surprises. And if God was pleased with his handiwork, so was I. My mother was only too glad to let me mind little Emily, and, very soon, my life was centred on her to the exclusion of all else — death and the grave, and the little pink doll from the Fair.

A Shelf-full of Dolls
A Doll for my Pocket

Most dolls' house families consisted of these 'little pink dolls with china heads', their varying sizes making them excellent for this purpose. An added charm lay in the variety of ways in which they could be dressed, the bigger ones as mothers and fathers, nurses, maids, butlers etc., the smaller ones as boys or girls according to choice. But the little dolls in the story, with their fate all ready planned, were not dressed at all.

Dolly Deaths

DOLLY DEATHS

W hen I was very young, my favourite pastime was playing at 'Death'. This is mixed up in my memory with my Saturday Penny, the 'Penny Bazaar' and my Dolls' House.

In those days, most children received a Saturday penny and most children squandered it forthwith on sweets, and who could blame them? The tempting variety of delectable items sweet shops had to offer then, for a penny or a ha'penny was more than any child could resist — huge brown humbugs, bulls' eyes, liquorice boot-laces, sugar sticks, aniseed balls, conversation lozenges, toffees, boiled sweets, there was no end to them. Even if your wealth amounted to no more than a farthing, you could still indulge in a tiny bar of chocolate!

However, not for me were the temptations of the sweet shop. My Saturday penny was reserved for the purchase of a little pink doll from the Penny Bazaar. Mother took me to the Penny Bazaar every Thursday, this being our shopping day. Well do I remember its all-pervading odour of carbolic soap that came wafting out to meet us as we approached its open doors. And well do I remember the wondrous array of articles of every description piled on the counters and suspended from lines overhead. But the toys were its chief attraction. Ranged behind a low brass trelliswork on a counter which seemed to run the whole lentgh of the shop were Noah's Arks, dolls, toy tea-sets, beads in little boxes with glass lids, humming tops, balls of every size and colour, picture books, painting books, bags of marbles, skipping ropes with plain or striped handles, shuttlecocks and battledores, whips and tops, dying pigs (balloons made in the shape of pigs which squeaked as they were let down), in fact everything that any child could desire. As I could neither see over nor through the trelliswork, Mother used to lift me up to make my choice which was always the same — a little pink doll with a china head.

I needed these little dolls for burying when I played at 'Death'. This was quite a complicated game requiring some preparation. First, I had to put the little doll to bed in the dolls' house, then I had to make blinds out of flour bags and stick them over the windows to denote a death within. (In those days, flour bags were made of thick, creamy-coloured paper very representative of linen blinds, and as flour was sold by the stone they were of a useful size). My glue was water which held the blinds in position for an adequate time.

My preparations completed, I would push Elizabeth, my big china doll round the playroom in her pram, starting off briskly but slowing down as I passed the dolls' house, to whisper softly, "Dear me, someone must have passed away, I wonder who it could be."

Then, I would set Elizabeth in her pram aside while I opened the dolls' house and removed the little doll from her bed. With no ceremony,—for I knew nothing about funerals, I would take her out into the garden and bury her, digging her grave with a tea-spoon I kept for the purpose.

Finally, I would return to the playroom take down the blinds from the windows of the dolls' house, and repeat the ritual of pushing Elizabeth round the room, this time, pausing to observe sadly, "They must have buried her then ... ah well ..."

This play made me glow with satisfaction, I had no pre-occupation with death, no secret fear of dying, in my play I was merely imitating my mother, making the same observations to Elizabeth as she made to me as she pushed me along in my go-cart. The little dolls were an accessory to make my play the more real. And how real it was! As I pushed Elizabeth round in her pram, I was no longer a little girl with her doll, but a mother with her child, dignified, knowledgeable and full of concern.

MY CELLULOID BABY

Wistered mother would have had me believe otherwise. Once, when arguing hen I was very young, I firmly believed my dolls were alive. My the point with my little friend Mabel, I had turned to her for support. "It's true, isn't it Mamma?" I said. "They are alive." And she had answered quite crossly, "You know they aren't."

But I knew better. How did they close their eyes if they were not alive? And how did my baby wet herself? My baby was a small celluloid doll which I loved the best of all my dolls because I could bath her. I didn't realize that while I bathed her, she filled with water and that this trickled out again through the holes in her legs.

One day I had positive proof that my baby was alive. 'The lions' that spasmodically charged through our playroom were responsible for this. These were the invention of my elder sister Monica, a bright child with a really frightening imagination. We had only recently moved into a new house and our playroom was next to the bathroom. Every now and then, without any warning, the room would vibrate with bloodcurdling roars and rattles which, of course, came from the bathroom cistern next door. I didn't know this and Monica took advantage of my ignorance to frighten me. "Quick", she would cry when the tumult began. "The lions! Hide your face! If they see you looking, they'll eat you!"

I never looked, so the lions never ate me but my poor baby looked and she was eaten completely. It happened on a day when she was wetter than usual and I had leant over the fireguard and put her on the hob to dry. When I raised my head after the intrusion of the lions, she had vanished! She had in fact, as Monica well knew, been eaten by the flames and not by the lions. "My baby's gone." I gasped.

"The lions have eaten her," said Monica. "She must have looked. She's in Heaven now. God will give her to a little dead girl to play with."

The thought of my precious baby in the arms of a little dead girl was more than I could bear and I began to cry. Mamma came into the playroom to see what was the matter and when I told her about the lions eating my baby, she was quite unsympathetic. "Your doll fell into the fire and was burnt," she said. "How many times have I told you not to go near the fire."

I continued to cry. It mattered little how my baby had perished, she was still in the arms of a little dead girl.

Monica never mentioned the lions again and a few days later when we all went into tea, there, sitting on the table beside my plate, was, I thought, my own little baby doll. "Has she come back?" I asked in astonishment.

"That's a new doll," explained Mamma, "and mind you don't put her near the fire."

I was overjoyed. God had given me a new baby just as he had given 'Mrs Hart across the road' a new one when her first one had died. How kind he was!

58

THE NEW WIG

I was an only child and dolls were my companions. Of these, I remember three especially, a very nice china doll called Elizabeth and two rather old wax dolls called Victoria and Veronica. These three dolls were 'sisters' and I was obsessed by the fear of hurting their feelings by not treating them all exactly the same. I went to the utmost pains to see that their hats and dresses were equally attractive and if I had only one of anything such as a necklace or a brooch, they had to take turns in wearing it. Being such a fair-minded child, you can imagine my concern when, one day, Mamma announced, "I think I'll get Elizabeth a new wig."

I knew Elizabeth was a superior doll but to single her out for a new wig would, I thought, hurt her sisters' feelings beyond measure. "Can't Victoria and Veronica have new wigs too?" I asked.

"No," said Mamma. "It doesn't matter about them, but Elizabeth is a very good doll." Such injustice was more than I could bear and I burst into tears. Mamma told be to stop being a silly little girl and went away, leaving me crying. If she had known why I was crying, she would have thought me sillier still!

In due course, Elizabeth appeared in a new and luxurious wig and I had to admit she looked lovely. But the wig was so thick and curly, it made Victoria's hair and Veronica's look meagre indeed. Mamma must have noticed this too, for she produced a length of scarlet ribbon and tied an enormous bow on the top of each of their heads. This evened things up miraculously, and I was overjoyed to think that the sisters' feelings had so happily been spared.

A SUNDAY TREAT

I was a London child and my summer holidays were spent visiting 'Grandmamma in the country'. Grandmamma lived in Surrey. She had a house covered with roses and honeysuckle and a garden which to me, used to a parched stretch of grass in a London square, seemed perfect paradise. It was full of little secret places I remember, where a child could play unobserved. I used to play at 'Ladies,' pretending I was grown up and visiting my friends. I would carry on animated conversations with them about their children, their operations and the servant problem.

However, the garden was not the chief attraction of my visits to Grandmamma. It was 'The Princess.' The Princess was a doll, but a very exceptional one. She was not a baby or a little girl but an elegant lady! She had come from Paris, and the exquisite clothes she wore had been made there too — all hand-sewn with the minutest of stitches. But it was not because of her clothes or the fact that she was of French extraction that The Princess impressed me. It was because she had belonged to my mother who had died when I was a baby. When Mamma had left home as a bride, Grandmamma had put the Princess away between sheets of tissue paper in her wardrobe drawer, and there she had lain undisturbed until I started my summer-time visits.

I was never allowed to play with The Princess, indeed I doubt if I could have played with her, she was so hard and stiff, but on Sundays, in the afternoon, when I was primly seated in the drawing room, Grandmamma would bring her to me and place her in my lap where I was permitted to hold her until tea-time. Then Grandmamma would re-wrap her in the tissue paper and take her upstairs again to her wardrobe drawer, there to remain until Sunday came round again.

This treat was the highlight of my visits to Grandmamma and made me feel, in some strange way, that I was visiting Mamma as well as Grandmamma. It made Sunday the very pleasantest day in the week for me instead of the dreariest, as it was at home.

A Doll of French Extraction like The Princess
A Sunday Treat

DOLLS' CLOTHES

I remember with great loathing the 'Sewing' lessons at the 'Board School' I attended as a child of about nine in 1900. They were heralded in by the storming of the 'Corner Shop' for halfpenny thimbles, for woe-betide those who arrived without this most essential piece of equipment! They were made to stand in a line in front of the class and hold out their hands for a flick of the cane. I was spared this because I always took the precaution of borrowing my mother's thimble. It was far too big for me, of course, and I had to remove it in order to sew, but it did serve to protect my dignity.

The lesson started with six hemming stitches. These, we had to execute on a scrap of cloth, dingy with much use. When we had finished our six stitches, we had to show them to Miss Harvey! If she was dissatisfied with them, we had to unpick them and do them again, but if she was satisfied, we proceeded to our 'garments.' These must have been petticoats or nightdresses, but all I remember about them were the 'run-and-fells' which we seemed constantly to be undoing. I became quite popular at one time through discovering a 'quick way' of undoing running stitches. I found that by snipping the two ends, it was possible to pull out the whole length of thread. I have a vision of a little girl, her pudgy face begrimed by tears, thrusting a crumpled mass into my arms and whispering, "Do it for me! Do it the quick way!" When eventually, we managed to finish our garments, we graduated to a frivolous bag or a mat with scalloped edges.

Doll's Clothes

One Saturday, as a treat, Mother took me with her to visit an Orphanage she was interested in. I was delighted with all I saw. The children, whom I had expected to be very dirty because they were poor, were so clean I remember thinking they looked as if they had been boiled! I was surprised also, to see how happy they were as I had imagined orphans to be too miserable to smile. But what impressed me most of all, was the sight of a group of little girls having a sewing lesson, for what do you think they were making? Not garments, not bags or mats, but dolls' clothes! There they were, making the daintiest little chemises, drawers, stays and petticoats and decorating them with lace and feather-stitching. I was filled with admiration. How lovely it would be I thought, if I could make a set of clothes like those for Letitia. Letitia was my doll and her clothes were in a sorry state from constant washing as, like most children I was very fond of having Wash Days! I pictured Letitia in her be-laced and feather-stitched underwear and Mother's friends turning up her dress to admire my handiwork. These pleasant thoughts prompted me to exclaim. "Oh Mamma, I wish we could make dolls' clothes in school."

"Well, why not suggest it to Miss Harvey?" replied Mamma, unaware of the enormity of her proposal, having been educated herself at a pleasant little private school. As if anyone would have the temerity to make an unsolicited remark to Miss Harvey! The very idea shocked me into silence.

However, Fate played into my hands and there came a day when I was to bring up the subject with Miss Harvey quite spontaneously. I had finished my garment and, after duly scrutinizing it, Miss Harvey said, "What would you like to make now, dear?"

Not realizing at the time that I was excpected to choose between a bag and a mat, I replied, "Some dolls' clothes, please."

Miss Harvey was bereft of speech. Such an outrageous request could never have been made before. She stared at me incredulously and, when at last, her power of speech returned, the angry words came tumbling out, "Dolls' clothes! You're at school, child! At school, do you understand! You don't come to school to play with dolls!... Go to your place!"

I went to my place and sat there, consumed with hatred for Miss Harvey and her thimbles, her hemming stitches, garments, bags and mats.

Years afterwards, I heard that Miss Harvey had died of an incurable disease. I also learned that all the time she had been teaching tiresome children, she had been in great pain, but couldn't give up because she had an invalid sister dependent on her. Poor Miss Harvey! Surely, to know all is to forgive all!

Cheap "Dutch" Dolls
broke all too easily
My China Doll

A Sixpence-ha'penny
Doll like Alice
My China Doll

MY CHINA DOLL

When I was young, china dolls were for the well-to-do, poor children like us played with wooden dolls, or rag dolls that we made ourselves. However, I did have a china doll, but I had to wait for her until I was fourteen years old!.

We were a poor family, how poor you may imagine when I tell you that my father had died leaving eight children! I was six at the time and there were two younger than me. Our mother made ends meet by dress-making and the earnings of the elder children as, one by one, they were able to leave school and find work. Needless to say, there was nothing to spend on luxuries such as new clothes, toys or presents, and we never had so much as a farthing to spend. But we accepted our lot and were happy enough, especially when we were sent to buy a 'cottage' loaf. This cost a penny farthing and if, after weighing it, the baker found that it did not come up to the standard weight of two pounds, he would cut a slice from another loaf to make up the deficiency, and this extra thick, crusty slice we were allowed to eat on our way home. What bliss that was and how we savoured every doughy morsel!

On Christmas Eve, we little ones hopefully hung our stockings up, but in the morning they would be as limp and empty as ever for Father Christmas never came down our chimney. Our elder brothers and sisters explained this away by telling us that such a fat old man couldn't possibly squeeze down our narrow chimney. However, Christmas didn't go unmarked for there was 'The Robins' Dinner' — a treat arranged by charitable ladies from the church. It was a wonderful event. We gathered in a happy rabble outside the Parish Hall long before 'Opening time' and when, at last, the doors were opened, we piled into a room gay with paper garlands and a huge shining Christmas tree surrounded by presents. The dinner was a very satisfying meal of pork pie and plum pudding, and afterwards, we sang carols with our minds on the presents. These were distributed without ceremony, we were just handed one suitable to our sex, as we left the Hall. Amongst the presents I received, two were outstanding — a tin tea set and a box of beads with a glass lid. Usually, like most of the girls, I was given a 'Dutch' doll. None of us liked these because, being of the very cheapest quality, their limbs snapped off as soon as we tried to move them. It was these unsatisfactory dolls that inspired me with a longing for a 'real' doll — a doll with a china face, hair, and proper arms and legs. None of my playmates possessed one but I often feasted my eyes on them in toyshop windows. I knew full well that there wasn't the slighest possibility of my ever being given such a doll, so I made a secret pact with myself that as soon as I was rich, I would buy myself a present of one.

I didn't reach this happy state until I was nearly fourteen years old and able to leave school. I went to work in the local biscuit factory and, being good at figures, I was put in the office where I spent my days working out lengthy sums. For this, I was paid five shillings a week, an enormous wage at that time. With what pride I presented my first five shillings to my mother! I felt I had allayed all her worries and that never again would she have to tussle with financial problems.

My mother gave me back sixpence for myself, and this, to a child who had never owned one farthing was wealth untold. At the first opportunity, I visited the nearest toyshop and joined the 'Club'. My longing for a real wax doll was about to be fulfilled! The shop was full of dolls and they all seemed magnificent to me. I remember being puzzled by the number of heads there were without any bodies. There were rows of them starting with enormous ones, and going down in descending size to quite minute ones. I didn't know that dolls' heads often got broken and could be replaced! After much deliberation, I made my choice — a flaxen-haired beauty with blue eyes, dressed in a white gown decorated with a little bow of blue ribbon. For this treasure, I agreed to pay a halfpenny a week into the 'Club', and after thirteen weeks the doll was to be mine.

As I was so busy, the weeks passed quickly and in no time at all, it seemed, I was bearing home my prize. I named the doll 'Alice' and although

I was too old to play with her, I loved her none the less. Strangely enough, I never made Alice any clothes, perhaps I thought I could not improve upon her white gown with its bow of blue ribbon! But I did make her an exquisite cradle from a boot box decorating it most lavishly with lace purchased at my own expense.

I continued to love Alice in the years that followed, even when I was a grown-up young lady, I still enjoyed lifting her out of her cradle and admiring her. But when finally, I was married and left home, I forsook my precious Alice. What became of her I do not know. I often wished I had kept her for my little daughter 'Olive'. But if Olive didn't inherit Alice, at least she inherited my love of dolls, and remembering my own doll-less days, I made sure she had a large and lovely family.

A SAD END

I never had but one doll, a great heavy wooden doll, no stuffing, no nice soft leather arms and legs. No! Its limbs were strongly wedged and pegged into its body. It was so big and heavy, I could scarcely drag it about (I was four years old only). Its name was 'Lummox'. I loved it but it was a nuisance to everyone else in the house. One unlucky day, I let it fall on my mother's foot and, in her pain and anger, she flung it on to the fire. And that was the end of Lummox.

Mary Anne Keeley
(Actress. Aged 87 in 1894)

GOD'S JUDGEMENT

I was quite old when I had diphtheria, I must have been eight or nine, so I can easily recall the details of my illness. I can remember the Doctor coming to take a swab of my throat and giving me an injection in my arm 'to be on the safe side.' A day or two later, he returned with the result of the swab and, as he came up to my bedroom with my mother, I heard him saying, "Yes, I'm afraid Nancy has the germ."

The Doctor sat by my bedside for quite a long time. He told me I would have to lie flat on my back and that meant having no pillow for my head. "It's the heart that is affected," he explained to my mother, and proceeded to regale her with stories of patients who had died from diphtheria through not understanding this. His recital ended with an account of the death of a little boy of about my own age. "He had, apparently, made a perfect recovery." he said, "and then one day when he was playing in the garden, he just fell over — dead!".

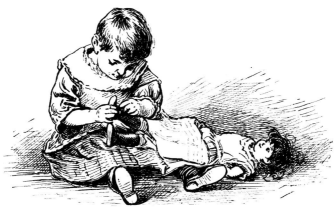

This story shocked me and from that day until long after I was better, I was continually feeling around for my heart to make sure that it was still beating.

As a reward for being a good girl and not making a fuss when my pillow was removed, Mother bought me a present of a little doll. She had movable arms and legs, a little china face that I could sponge and very fine, curly hair that I was pleased to find I could comb without it coming out. I loved the little doll, her smallness appealed to me and the fact that she wore a nightdress just like mine, because, of course, she too had diphtheria and had to stay in bed. I named the doll 'Olive', I don't know why, and Julia, my almost grown-up sister who had made the nightdress, promised to make her a frock to wear when she was well enough to get up.

In time, both Olive and I were allowed to get up and Julia produced the promised frock. It was made of green cashmere and decorated with French knots in thick shining, red silk. There was a little petticoat too, and a tiny pair of drawers with lace round the legs. I was entranced by everything and could hardly wait for the time to come when I would be able to show Olive to my little playmate, Effie. But, oh dear, a great shock was in store for me. When my six weeks' quarantine were over, Mother said, "The Doctor says that everything you have handled must be destroyed — books, toys, dolls, EVERYTHING." She gave me a box to put the things in because 'the men' would be coming for them any time.

I was utterly dismayed at the thought of losing Olive. I couldn't bear to part with her and so, without saying anything to anyone, I hid her in the dolls' house in the nursery. After that, my moments with Olive were stolen ones. I couldn't play with her anymore, I could only take her out when I thought no-one was about. But one glorious day, Effie arrived to play with me. Now, at last, I would be able to show her my treasure. "I've got something to show you, Effie," I said. "Hide you eyes and don't look until I tell you".

With that, I tiptoed over to the dolls' house and took Olive out. I held her out towards Effie and was just about to say 'Look!' when Paddy, our little Irish Terrier came bounding into the room. He must have thought Olive was a bone I was holding out to him and, grabbing her in his mouth, he made off with her down the stairs. Effie and I dashed after him shouting, "Paddy! Paddy!".

Out into the garden we raced, but before we had time to catch the little rascal, Mother came flying after us crying, "Nancy! Nancy! Stop!"

The urgency of her cries compelled me to stop and in a moment she was clasping me in her arms, fearing, I am sure, that I was about to drop down dead. "Oh," she gasped, "have you forgotten what the Doctor said about your heart?"

"But my doll," I sobbed, fogetting that the doll was the fugitive Olive.

"Never mind the doll," said Mother, leading me back to the house with Effie following also in tears, "you are more precious than any doll."

Olive was gone for ever. Her tragic end, I decided, was the will of God "from Whom no secrets are hid." Aware of my disobedience, He was obliged to punish me, but need He have been quite so thorough, I wondered.

SCARLETINA

I have very little hair now for I am well past my three-score years and ten, but when I was a child, my hair was thick and long and curly. I know it was pretty because people used to fondle it and once, when I was at a party, a lady referred to me as 'the little girl with the beautiful hair!' I have never forgotten this remark because my mother was so angry when I told her about it. It was when she was brushing my hair the same night that I said quite casually, "A lady at the party called me 'the little girl with the beautiful hair'." At this, Mamma stopped dead in her ministrations, and to my complete astonishment, announced angrily, "This hair is not yours. It is God's. Remember that."

I puzzled over Mamma's words for a long time wondering how my hair wasn't mine and, at length, I arrived at the only possible solution: God had lent me my hair! But what if He were to decide to take it back? I would have no hair at all then. I couldn't imagine what it would be like to have no hair, but I was to know soon enough, for shortly after this, I got Scarlet Fever or 'Scarletina' as it was called in those days, and my head was shorn of its long, thick curls.

I remember the day I was taken ill very well for it was on the same day that I discovered Mamma could see out of the back of her head, a fact as fascinating as her ability to push a hat-pin right through her head without wincing. I had taken Angela, my doll, into the dining-room to show Mamma, because I had re-dressed her and thought she looked very smart. "Look Mamma!" I said. "Do you like Angela?"

Mamma had her back to me, she was kneeling down settling the fire, and without turning her head, murmured appreciatively, "Oh, yes."

"But you're not looking, Mamma," I protested.

73

"No, but I can see," came the answer.

Fancy, I thought, when you are grown-up like Mamma you can see out of the back of your head!

If she had troubled to turn her head she would, no doubt, have noticed my feverish appearance. I remember how hot I felt at the time and how my head ached. But I didn't complain, you never did in those days, you waited for someone to notice you were ill.

In the end, I suppose, I must have been put to bed and I know I was very ill for some time. The Doctor ordered my hair to be cut off and mother complied. I didn't protest for I was too ill to care what she did. It wasn't until I was very much better that I caught a glimpse of myself in the looking glass. I was horrified at my ugliness and cried bitterly, but all Mamma said was, "Your hair had to be cut off to make you better."

For days afterwards, my life was a misery. I discussed the situation with Angela, envying her long, flaxen curls. Then, one day, in a frenzy of jealousy, I ruthlessly chopped off her curls, making her as ugly as I was myself. How could I have done such a thing to the doll that I adored! However, this ruthless act was to be my salvation. When Mamma saw Angela, she was highly displeased. "You have ruined her," she said. "Your hair will grow again, but the doll's . . . !"

My mother's words were as music in my ears. My hair would grow again! I had never thought of that! I wasn't going to be ugly for ever and ever. I could forget about my hair and as for Angela, why, she could wear a bonnet! Dolls wore bonnets both indoors and out, so no-one need ever know she had lost her curls. I wouldn't tell anyone and Angela certainly wouldn't.

ACKNOWLEDGEMENTS

I should like to express my thanks to all the friends who have shared their 'dolly' experiences with me, and especially to Dora Fielding, Mary Birchall, Doreen Smith, Heather Barclay, Kathleen Staton, Ivy Allen and Margaret Hewitt who have entrusted their most precious dolls to my care, and also to the late Alec Buckels who shared my enthusiasm for Victorian dolls.

I gratefully acknowledge also, the careful and sympathetic co-operation of the publishers; David Mitchell and George Power; the photographers, Seaman's of Chesterfield; and the cover designer.

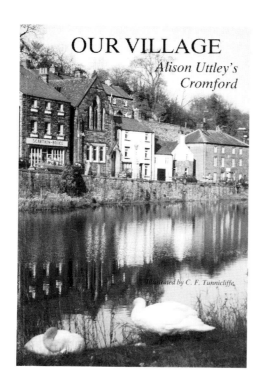

To the Reader

If you have enjoyed these stories you will probably also be pleased by our Alison Uttley Centenary book (1984) entitled OUR VILLAGE: ALISON UTTLEY'S CROMFORD. This is a collection by Jaqueline Mitchell of Alison Uttley's essays recalling the village of her childhood. The delightful illustrations by C. F. Tunnicliffe are taken from the original publications, now almost all out of print. The book is a quality paperback, with full-colour cover, priced at £2.85.

Reminiscence of a different kind and of a more recent period appears in THE CRICH TALES: UNEXPURGATED ECHOES FROM A DERBYSHIRE VILLAGE. These were collected by Dr. Geoffrey Dawes, in the King's Arms, in Crich, home of the National Tramway Museum. Truly Chaucerian in many respects, the tales exemplify the earthy humour and rustic shrewdness of Derbyshire villagers of a bygone generation. Evocative illustrations by Geoff Taylor, notes on the social history of the village, and a simple dialect glossary complete this very enjoyable book which costs £2.85.

"A Good Child's Present" is how we ambiguously describe JOURNEY FROM DARKNESS. Unlike many contemporary children's stories it does not deal with acute social problems nor gratuitous violence. The story is suitable for children of 8-12. It is set in 1860, and is about a pit-boy, Peter, who rescues his lame pony from the slaughterman and sets out for his uncle's farm in the Peak District to get help. Unexpectedly, his uncle needs Peter's help too. Jane Inglis, writing in The School Librarian, calls the book "a well-told tale with a satisfying shape and a sprightly succession of incidents ... the conditions in Victorian colliery and countryside are lightly but convincingly drawn." The author, Gordon Ottewell, once a Derbyshire mining engineer, is now a headteacher, and knows his subject and his readers. The book is enhanced by highly-praised pictures by Geoff Taylor, and costs £1.95.

The Peak District of Derbyshire is still today the scene of many journeys on foot, — now by people walking for pleasure. For those who perforce live in built-up districts it evokes a memory of lost landscapes, and for children it can arouse an exciting affinity with wild nature. Gruelling hikes, however, are not within everyone's capabilities, and this is one reason why Norman Taylor's FAMILY WALKS IN THE WHITE PEAK was hailed in the Great Outdoors as " ... quite simply, the best Peak District short walks guide yet published." Taking in the most beautiful of the Derbyshire Dales, each of the sixteen circular walks has a pub welcoming children, or a teashop en route, which means also that "rescue" by car can be arranged if necessary. Maps and route descriptions are on facing pages, and there are notes on wildlife, buildings and children's activities — rocks to climb, caves to explore, or streams to dabble in. Compiled by a teacher and parent with children very much in mind, the walks are also ideal for anyone who by necessity or choice prefers a moderate challenge, with easy gradients and occasional rest-stops. Enlivened with many photographs and line-drawings, Family Walks in the White Peak costs £1.95.

BOOKS by LILIAN McCREA

OXFORD UNIVERSITY PRESS
Stories To Tell In The Nursery School
Stories To Play In The Infant School
Puppets And Puppet Plays
Story-telling (OXFORD JUNIOR ENCYCLOPAEDIA — Article)

SIR ISAAC PITMAN AND SON LTD.
A Calendar Of Stories
Round The Year In Prayer And Story
Polish Folk Tales And Legends
Twelve Puppet Plays

E. J. ARNOLD AND SON LTD.
Irish Fireside Stories
Animal Scrapbook

CULTURAL PUBLICATIONS
A Pocketful Of Stories
All Sorts Of Stories And Verses

Stories and verses reproduced in the Puffin Books and Ladybird Books, contributed to 'Child Education' and broadcast in Australia and New Zealand.

The publishers welcome ideas and manuscripts relating to Derbyshire, or with a specialised appeal extending beyond the county.

Scarthin Books of Cromford are the leading Peak District specialists in secondhand and antiquarian books, and are always ready to purchase large or small collections of good books and music, ancient or modern.
Contact: Dr. D. J. Mitchell by letter, or phone Wirksworth 3272.